Business Law and Practice

SHAREHOLDERS AND SHARE CAPITAL

Question and suggested answers

Written by Steve Norton

GW00496973

i

Dedicated to Leah and Barbara

ACKNOWLEDGMENTS

I would like to thank all staff from the London Metropolitan University for the learning experience and knowledge gained to write this book and choice of learning materials I used to produce this guides based on my own notes. I would also like to thank the students who shared that learning experience with me.

CONTENTS

1. INTRODUCTION

I wrote this book as an aid to those like me who have studied this subject area on the Legal Practice Course (LPC) or are intending to in the near future. I have tried to produce a number of questions and suggested answers based on information from my own notes and studies which I hope existing or potential LPC students will find useful as a study guide which is based around typical exam questions.

This is the another short guide in a series of books initially covering subject areas within the Business Law and Practice (BLP) core module. I have material for other similar books on this core subject area of the LPC and depending on interest may consider producing other short guide books broken down into other bitesize chunks for easier digestion (continuing with the metaphor) of the overall subject areas. I have not seen any similar short LPC guides of this kind in my searches so I hope this fills a gap in the market.

This particular volume deals with the issue of share holders and share capital.

2. SUBJECT OUTLINE

ROLE OF SHAREHOLDERS

DECISION MAKING
PROCESS

SHAREHOLDER
AGREEMENTS

This guide aims to deal in question and answer form with the important role of shareholders in running a private limited company in the first main chapter 3. Chapter 4 sets out a series of questions and suggested answers covering the important area of share capital which has been referred to as the *life blood* of a company.

This book hopes to add more pieces in the jigsaw puzzle of the Business Law and Practice core module on the Legal Practice Course.

3. ROLE OF SHAREHOLDERS

QUESTIONS AND SUGGESTED ANSWERS

QUESTION 1

WHAT ARE SHAREHOLDERS?

SUGGESTED ANSWER

Shareholders own the company and the assets. Major decisions for the company are made through shareholder general meetings.

QUESTION 2

HOW DO YOU BECOME A SHAREHOLDER?

SUGGESTED ANSWER

- On incorporation of the company
- On the issue of new shares
- On a transfer of shares

QUESTION 3

HOW MANY TYPES OF SHARES ARE THERE?

SUGGESTED ANSWER

There are two main types of shares:
Preference shares and Ordinary shares.

QUESTION 4

HOW DO SHAREHOLDERS MAKE DECISIONS?

SUGGESTED ANSWER

Shareholders make decisions through resolutions at shareholder general meeting passing <u>Ordinary</u> or <u>Special</u> resolutions.

QUESTION 5

WOULD A DECISION TO EMPLOY A NEW MEMBER OF STAFF SUCH AS A PART TIME JUNIOR ADMINISTRATOR REQUIRE A SHAREHOLDER'S MEETING?

SUGGESTED ANSWER

No, not usually as this is a small financial commitment and would be in the remit of directors on their own.

QUESTION 6

JUNK FOOD LTD WANT TO EMPLOY AN ACCOUNTANT ON A LARGE SALARY OF £100,000 ON A FIXED-TERM CONTRACT, WOULD THIS REQUIRE A SHAREHOLDER'S MEETING?

SUGGESTED ANSWER

Yes more likely as this is a large financial commitment and would need a shareholder's meeting to get approved.

QUESTION 7

HOW IS VOTING ON RESOLUTIONS CONDUCTED AT A DIRECTOR'S MEETING?

SUGGESTED ANSWER

Directors only have one vote each and decisions are made by straightforward majority of votes.

QUESTION 8

HOW IS VOTING CONDUCTED AT A SHAREHOLDER'S MEETINGS?

SUGGESTED ANSWER

In shareholder meetings the voting can be on a majority voting of those at the meeting or a "poll vote" may be called for on a resolution. This then depends how many shares each voter holds in the company. This will then depend not on the number of hands voting, but instead on the number of shares each voter has in the company.

QUESTION 9

WHAT IS THE DIFFERENCE BETWEEN AN ORDINARY AND A SPECIAL RESOLUTION?

SUGGESTED ANSWER

Examples of resolutions needed for different decisions

<u>Ordinary resolutions</u> are used for the following decisions:-

- Approval of a director's service contract over 2 years (s.188 Companies Act 2006)
- Approving a substantial property transaction (non-cash assets worth over £5,000 or over 10% of the company's net assets – s.190 Companies Act 2006).

<u>Special resolutions</u> are used for the following decisions:-

- Changing the constitution of the company through the articles of association.

- Changing a company name (Companies Act 2006 s,77(1)
- Disapplying the shareholder's pre-emption rights. A special resolution is required to change the right under s.561 of the Companies Act 2006 which provides

that if a company issues new shares, the existing shareholders have the first right to to buy those new share in the same proportion as their existing share holding. Example – If you own 52% of shares you could buy shares up to that amount. This prevention right can be disapplied where a company is a private limited company with only one class of shares wishing to allot shares without complying with s.561 using s. 569 of the Companies Act 2006.

QUESTION 10

IS VOTING THE SAME FOR ORDINARY AND SPECIAL RESOLUTIONS AT SHAREHOLDER MEETINGS INVOLVING A POLL VOTE?

SUGGESTED ANSWER

No, the voting percentage needed to pass and ordinary or special resolution differs. An ordinary resolution requires *more than* 50% of shares of those voting to pass the vote. A special resolution requires 75% of the total shares of those voting but if those at the meeting holding 25% shares vote against the resolution it will fall.

QUESTION 11

HOW ARE SHAREHOLDER'S MEETINGS ORGANISED?

SUGGESTED ANSWER

- Any director can call a Board Meeting giving reasonable notice
- Directors meet and decide to convene a General Meeting

- Directors convene General Meeting giving 14 days notice (small companies can use short notice)
- Shareholders hold General Meeting and pass special/ordinary resolution/s
- Directors file at Companies House.
- May need to reconvene Board Meeting to discuss any resolutions passed at the General Meeting
- Minutes of meeting taken to record resolutions passed people who attended any other important decisions taken.

QUESTION 12

What is the difference between the term "member" and "shareholder"?

SUGGESTED ANSWER

The expression "shareholder" and "member" are often used interchangeably but members. There are some subtle differences:-

• Members are shareholders who have their names enter on the register of members

• Only members can vote on ordinary and special resolutions and receive dividends

• You become a shareholder *before* you become a member

• Purchasing shares will make you a shareholder but not automatically make you a member. S. 112 Companies Act 2006 provides that a person will become a member of the company once he/she has agreed to become a member and their name has been entered on the register of members.

QUESTION 12

WHAT IS A SHAREHOLDER AGREEMENT AND IS IT USEFUL?

SUGGESTED ANSWER

A shareholders' agreement is an agreement between the shareholders of a company. It can be between all shareholders or only some of the shareholders (maybe based on holding the same type of share). It can be used to protect the shareholders' investment or interest in the company and to establish a fair relationship between the shareholders and govern how the company is run.

A shareholder's agreement may:-

Set out the shareholders' rights and obligations;

• Regulate the sale of shares in the company;

• Set out how the company is going to be run;

- Provide an element of protection for minority shareholders and the company; and
- Define how important decisions are to be made.

4. SHARE CAPITAL

QUESTIONS AND SUGGESTED ANSWERS

WHAT IS SHARE
CAPITAL?

CLASSES OF
SHARES

ISSUING OF SHARES

PROCEDURAL
ISSUES

QUESTION 1

WHAT IS SHARE CAPITAL?

SUGGESTED ANSWER

Share capital is known as the life blood of the company. Share capital is the money invested in a company by the shareholders. Share capital is a long-term source of finance and in return for their investment shareholders gain a share of the ownership of the company.

QUESTION 2

WHAT ARE THE MAIN CLASSES OF SHARES?

SUGGESTED ANSWER

There are two main types of shares. <u>Ordinary</u> and <u>Preference</u> shares. Ordinary shares carry voting rights. Preference shares may carry voting rights but the distinguishing point is pref. shares pay a dividend of a certain fixed percentage – maybe 5-6% where the company makes a profit and a dividend declared. The ordinary shareholder may not benefit from this but where the company has a good year and makes a substantial profit the ordinary shareholder could get a better return on his/her investment. Partly paid shares are in large public companies and you pay part of the money of the shares. Where a company goes into liquidation you could still be liable for the balance owed on your shares. That is the limit of your liability in limited companies. Shares at a discount are illegal – shares cannot be issued at a price below their nominal value. Shares at a premium are used in a successful company where shares are sold at a premium over and above their nominal value.

QUESTION 3

HOW ARE SHARES ISSUES?

SUGGESTED ANSWER

When shares are issued this means *new shares* created in the company unlike a transfer of shares which involves selling *existing shares* in a company. The company's internal registers must be kept up to date in these situations. If I sell 600 shares to another shareholder in the company it will need to be registered that person has 600 more shares and I have 600 less. The debit and cash accounts need to be updated. In liquidation outside creditors come first above shareholders when funds distributed.

QUESTION 4

WHAT ARE DIVIDENDS?

SUGGESTED ANSWER

A <u>dividend</u> is a payment a company can make to shareholders if it has made a profit. A company pays corporation tax on the profits and the recipient pays income tax on any dividends. A company cannot count dividends as business costs when you they work out their Corporation Tax. Directors can recommend a dividend but shareholders have to approve a dividend of the same or less than the amount the director has recommended, not more. A company must not pay out more in dividends than its available profits from current and previous financial years.

QUESTION 5

IS THERE A RESTRICTION ON SHARE CAPITAL?

SUGGESTED ANSWER

Under the Companies Act 1985 when a company was incorporated it had to state an amount of authorised share capital of a particular amount and to increase this you needed a resolution. The Companies Act 2006 ended this and a company has authority to issue share where there is only one type of share. The only issue now are the pre-emption rights.

QUESTION 6

DO DIRECTORS HAVE THE POWER TO ISSUE SHARES?

SUGGESTED ANSWER

The Companies Act 2006 give the director's the power to issue shares (s.550 Companies Act 2006). Under the model articles there are no restrictions on issuing shares. Sometimes in smaller private companies other shareholders may want to restrict the issue of shares to certain people.

QUESTION 7

WHAT ARE THE STATUTORY PRE-EMPTION RIGHTS?

SUGGESTED ANSWER

S.561 Companies Act 2006 provides if new shares issued/created it has to first offer new shares to existing shareholders in the same proportion they own shares. Example – A has 60% of shares in the company and the company issues a new batch of shares. A has the right to purchase 60% of those shares if they have they funds and wish to. A can waive their pre-emption rights or exercise them. Problems may arise where the company issues new shares but not in exactly the same proportion people hold them in the company. You can disapply your pre-emption rights if you do not want to be restricted to applying for the same proportion of shares and may possibly want more. You would need to get a <u>special resolution</u> passed at a General Meeting of shareholders to disapply the pre-emption rights and enable shares to be issued in *different proportions*. There is an option to pass a resolution to disapply pre-emption rights on a particular occasion or from here on, every time new shares are issued. <u>S.561</u> applies if new shares are being issued for cash only. If someone has for instance an expensive car this would not invoke pre-emption rights as this involves non cash payment for shares. <u>S.569</u> Companies Act 2006 deals with passing a special resolution to disapply pre-emption rights.

QUESTION 8

CAN A COMPANY RESTRICT THE TRANSFER OF NEW SHARES?

SUGGESTED ANSWER

Where a company wants to restrict transfer of new shares it must be specifically dealt with in it's articles of association. A company can include a provision in its articles to prevent the transfer of shares by not allowing certain people to be entered on the company's register of members. Another option is to have a Shareholders Agreement that in the event one shareholder decides to sell their shares there is agreement how they are sold, such as having to sell to existing shareholders.

ABOUT THE AUTHOR

I have studied law for many years as a part time
student and have both undergraduate and post
graduate qualifications and have completed the LPC.
Outside of my day job I have worked in volunteer
legal support roles offering advice and assistance. I
maintain a keen interest in legal study in particular,
as well as other areas of study.

ISBN: 978-1790988334

Printed in Great Britain
by Amazon